ETHAN LEWIS

TAKE FIVES

SHORT STUDIES IN PENTAMETER

UNIVERSITY PRESS OF THE SOUTH

2022

Copyright 2022 by Ethan Lewis.

All rights reserved. No part of this publication may be reproduced, stored in a retrieval system, or transmitted, in any form or by any means, electronic, mechanical, photocopying, recording or otherwise, without the prior written permission of the Publisher.

Published in the United States by The University Press of the South. Printed in France.

E-mail: universitypresssouth@gmail.com

Visit our award-winning web pages: www.unprsouth.com
www.punouveaumonde.com

Ethan Lewis.
Take Fives. Short Studies in Pentameter.
Foreword by Alain Saint-Saëns.
First English Edition. Poetry Series, 36.

x, 176 pages.

Front Cover Art: George Delamotte, "A Country Lane with a Farm Labourer Climbing a Five-bar Gate," Yale Center for British Art, Paul Mellon Collection. Photo by the Yale Center for British Art. Image in the public domain.

Front Cover Design by Stan Levêque. Reproduced with Permission.
Interior design by Mark Pence.

1. Poetry. 2. American Poetry. 3. Lyric Sketches. 4. Epistemology. 5. Nature. 6. Tributes. 7. Prosody. 8. Religious Poetry. 9. Alain Saint-Saëns. 10. Ethan Lewis.

ISBN: 978-1-952799-45-7
2022

*In Memoriam, samBdavis,
Il miglior scrittore.*

CONTENTS

Foreword xi

MISCELLANY 1
   A.M. 1
   Sundry Morning 2
   Wynds 3
   Coy Comfort 4
   Fearful Symmetry 5
   Black Hawk 6
   A Subtle Rite 7
   Crop Up the Band 8
   For Jacqueline and Marcellus 9
   Extra Innings 10
   June Ode 11
   Tombeau d'Anton Bruckner 12
   Of Intervals 13
   Homeric Hymn 14
   After Her Orchestration 15
   Tafelmusik 16
   Valentine 17
   Then 18
   Epithalamion 19
   Marconi in March 20
   Gavotte 21
   Aquarelle 22
   Who Comes to Call No Cause for "Who Ya Gonna Call" 23
   Spielberg among the Conifers 24
   Statues on the Capitol Mall 25
      The Monitor 25
      "My competitor in top of all design" 26
      Memento 27
   Eternal Matinee 28
   That Day You Departed 29
   Measurements 30
   To Seventeen 31
   Violincello 32
   Memorial 33

NATURA NATURANS 35
    Shouldering the Weather 36
    Discretion Is 37
    Snolytka 38
    "*Nel foco che li affina*" 39
    Reprieve 40
    Vernal Prelude 41
    Garden Harbinger 42
    March 43
    Fair Fowl Weather 44
    Medleyed 45
    Paired in the Palette of March 46
    Cat at the Window 47
    Cat and Cactus 48
    Bast 49
    From Her Bird Seat 50
    Crochat 51
    Cupidi(kit)ty 52
    Tandem Nap 53
    Corollae 54
    Spring Chiaroscuro 55
    A Momentary Petal Dispensation 56
    Mnemonic 57
    Viola Tricolor Tough Guy 58
    Augury 59
    Trumpet Vines 60
    Not Much Ado, yet Something 61
    Spelled with a Y 62
    Potted Panopticon 63
    Tractatus Hydrangeas 64
    Edeladweiss, or Fleur-de-lycee 65
    Not Always 66
    Elevenish Caprice 67
    Obcidatus 68
    Etiolate 69
    Southwestern Sojourn 70

Train 71
Sunny Morning at Sonoma Estates 72
Under Sun Instead of Glass 73
Urban Avian 74
Vulgivagus Cavia Porcellus 75
Hare Brain 76
Parvum Addendum 77
Adagio 78
Two Montpeliar Portraits 79
Tornado Watch 80
Savannahs 81
N.N. (reprise) 82
Four Seasons 83
Sennet 84
"A nameless air" 85
Autumn Denouement 86
Thaw Thought 87
Entomologous 88
Dome 89
The Rain Reminds Me 90
Many Beds in His Garden 91

HOMAGE THROUGH HOPKINS AND HERBERT 93

Circumambient 94
Installations 95
A Chapel in Santa Fe 96
Laudatus Two 97
Notre Dame 98
Might 99
Kafka's Psalm 100
Matthew 10:29 101
Transport 102
Summa contra Gentiles 103
Paying Forward 104
Noel 2019 105
(*Goddamn* 105

TRAGICOMIC ENTR'ACTE 107
 Airport Prayer 107
 Michael and Martha (and Me) 108
 Seventh Stage 109
 Mutandis Mutandis 110
 Blank Study 111
 "Well Done, Thou Good and Faithful Servant" 112
 The Collector 113
 Homage to Nicolas Jensen (and Mark Pence) 114

HARVARD VERSES 115
 Composed in Harvard Yard 115
 Pine in the Sand 116
 Back Then Again 117
 A Lob's Length from the Lab 118
 Chiseled Motto Addendum 119
 On the Waters 120
 Coterie Redux 121

BUT SOMETIMES THE SNIDE'S ON YOU: POEMS PEEVISH 123
 Unrequited 123
 Far Better Fared So 124
 Our Taste for the Taboo 125
 Away With It 126
 Purge for Pelf 127
 Incredulously Crass 128
 Cropped Out 129
 Democratic Doggerel 130
 What Moss Can't Cover Up 131
 Climacteric 132
 Not Answering the Bell 133
 Wilmot, of Rochester, Challenged by a Peer 134
 Found on a Flyleaf of *Gulliver's Travels* 135

SMALL WONDERS 137

    Equinocturne 137
    Upon Looking into Wallace Stevens 138
    For Edward Lear and Virginia Woolf 139
    Billy Pilgrim's Progress 140
    Ever After, Daddio 141
    Casa Blancamericana 142
    Musk, Lamp, Memory 143
    Parentheses 144
    In Praise of Spooner 145
  Who's Who Was 146
  The Game's Aglove 147
    On a Recent Discovery Pertaining to Our Origins 148
    Reverie, and Homage, at Thirty Thousand Feet 149
  Tangeil Dhut, P.M.D. 150
  Translation 151
    First Little Piggy 152
    Two Faults 153
    The Geese at UIS 154
    Small Wonder 155
    Tuesday (not the Third Day) 156
    What Beats All 157
    What Goes Round 158
    Motions Recollected in Tranquility 159
    Done (Donne): Gone 160
    Near Sugarloaf 161
    Strange Meeting 162
    Semper Fraternitas 163

About the Poet 165

An Apologia by way of Afterword 167

CODA: Mid-Length Playfully Personal Study in Pentameter;
    Late December, 2021 169

FOREWORD

Ethan Lewis,
Poet Laureate of Hawthorne Place

Ethan Lewis, dubbed "Poet Laureate of Hawthorne Place," writes daily, stopped only perhaps by night time: "But then again, bed beckons: 'It is time. / You satisfied exigencies of rhyme.'" Doesn't he declare, "Pentameter helps pass the time"? Maybe it is a way for him to keep away, at least for a while, "our fate: to disappear"; and does he know how to cry for a departed friend: "Our loss: your gentle soul and kindest life." Ethan Lewis does not ignore what he owes to other poets before him, whom he cites: William Blake, William Shakespeare, Homer, Charles Baudelaire, Ezra Pound, Emily Dickinson, Robert Burns, John Wilmot, and so many others. Time is passing, but "rhymes sill limn the present century." Ethan Lewis admits "the objective subjectivity of time" and, as a lucid poet, plays with it. Love comes and goes, but, as a visionary, Ethan Lewis can state: "I presage a renaissance of love." Music inhabits his poems, and he celebrates many composers who have influenced him, from Sebastian Bach to Anton Bruckner, Charpentier to Corelli, Mendelssohn, with a deep knowledge and a bright kindness.

As a man living in Springfield, Ethan Lewis purposely writes poems about Chicago and O'Hare Airport, and about the whole state of Illinois. At times, they echo the Galesburg, Illinois poet Carl Sandburg's immortal poem, *Chicago*, and some of the most beautiful poems by Ethan Lewis' colleague and poet, and friend, Rosina

Neginsky, in her book of poems, *Juggler*. Days, months, seasons, flow with their cortege of light, tornado watch, and snow, trees' leaves and birds' feathers: "So sun and rain and time will have their way." The nature loving poet is not fooled, though, and is clearly conscious of all the degradations made by man to his beloved trees. Two words to shout his distress, "It stings," maybe not to say more prosaically that "it stinks." Even used, then abandoned, Christmas trees sadden him: "I'd like to think somewhere a sacred wood / Keeps evergreen those needled that had stood."

Ethan Lewis loves his cats, be they "at the window," or gone "elsewhere to explore," faithful and dignified companions of his daily life. He likes their sense of restrained humor, their definite search for freedom, no doubt a "strong argument that cats shall enter heaven." He respects and honors his parents, too. He shows with an economy of words how hard it is to watch them slowly vanish away, vanquished as they are by dementia coming with age: "What does she still remember?" As a God fearing, loving son, he feels allowed to pray the Lord for mercy: "Could we […] beg an amnesty from ills of age, / And just grow older simply, pain assuage?" Ethan Lewis is a melancholic and proud poet, who dares speak on behalf of his fellow human beings and does it magnificently. He certainly personifies what poetry is and what makes a poet; he says it loudly: "Enough. […]Even in Hyvee the muse might call us."

ALAIN SAINT-SAËNS
Poet and Literary Critic

MISCELLANY

A.M.

My pentameter antenna fails to detect
KPOE these days, though I suspect
The trouble's due to battery depletion—
Which would explain as well the incompletion
Of incipient airs that, darting in mind's ear,
Don't wane so much as simply disappear.
Yet rather than replace my double-A's
To charge this lyric radio malaise,
Perhaps it behooves that I shift to an electric
Source and channel measures more eclectic.
But habit likely hardens the resistor,
Such that I'll keep on tuning my transistor.

Sundry Morning

Dubbed Poet Laureate of Hawthorne Place,
The lyric pressure's on to keep apace.
And when she tells her students, "He writes poems,"
I fancy a prosodic Sherlock Holmes
Observing the quotidian to limn
A mystery that solves the ear and mind.
At times, I must concede, it feels a curse,
Compelled to daily cogitate a verse:
To frame mundane experience in rhyme;
Yet when occasion haps on the sublime
Ignoring invocation seems a crime.
(Besides, pentameter helps pass the time.)

Wynds

Sometimes on walks I take back alley ways.
The nether side of high rises betrays
An urban secrecy that whispers, *where*
In front an ordered chaos reigns, back here
In shadow, stray pedestrians can find
A brief asylum. Alleys ease the mind.
And then the concrete corridors lead out
To crowded squares of wariness and doubt.

Coy Comfort

To court the dream of world enough, and time,
I *won't* deign to decide which way to walk;
Responsibilities I'll briefly mock,
And like Marvell hypothesize in rhyme.
But like him, too, I can't escape the clock.
Regardless where, my footsteps merely mime
On ground his symbol soaring through the air
That eternized our fate: to disappear.

Cf. Andrew Marvell, "To His Coy Mistress," ll. 1-4; 21-4.

Fearful Symmetry

First Pres' green stained glass and bright red door
Invite us in to learn what God is for.
But I can read the news on city streets,
And it's not good. A homeless man entreats
For change, with cup in hand. When William Blake
Composed *Songs of Experience* to slake
His thirst for right, he must have known
That, even in the chance wake of renown,
Impassioned remonstrations cast in verse
Could not prevent his London growing worse
For many. Each succeeding century
His rhymes still limn the present penury.

Cf. Blake, *Songs of Innocence and Experience*; "The Tyger."

Black Hawk

Courage is unafraid to weep or pray;
Nor need one know to whom the prayer's addressed.
Moreover, let the tears fall where they may:
All authenticity of feeling's blessed.
The stalwart soul perennially quests
Toward ascertainment of a juster day—
Embrace of commonsense displacing outrage,
Prepared by what comprises acts of courage.

A Subtle Rite

Russillo's quartet squared its audience,
Though didn't seem to care, and nor did we.
A private concert, on the contrary,
Mark crooning "Cheek-to-Cheek" that we might dance
Alone together in the tiny hall—
No strobe, or sequins shearing from a ball;
Instead, a pale, sepia shade of light
Embracing six within a winter night,
Illumed the moment of a subtle rite.

Crop Up The Band

Here on the Plains we harvest wheat and wind.
The threshers in the sky emit no sound,
Whereas the mechanisms on the ground
Snick systematically, in syncopation
To the tuneless orchestration of John Deere;
The mills, to choreography of air.

For Jacqueline and Marcellus

The cala lily set beside the lamp
Converts the desk into an avenue.
Beneath their lights night's thoughts stroll with a view
To print the next day's doings with their stamp.
Nothing so grand as setting the world on fire,
Or penning manifestoes to the crowds,
Or shaking down loud thunder from dark clouds;
To craft a sonnet, all that I desire.

I dim the lamp, yet still the lily glows,
As though to signal sleep some hours away.
There's verse to turn; the cogitant must stay
Until he brings this etude to a close.
    But then again, bed beckons, "It is time.
    You satisfied exigencies of rhyme."

"I spent last Saturday getting the fields ready—raking leaves, cleaning the concession stand, picking up dead rabbits off the infield… Now it's time to enjoy some ball!"

Extra Innings
(for Kara McElrath)

She extricates dead hares from fields near Danville
So sons can swing. The mother of Maranville
Might well have done the same, the shortstop's nickname
Notwithstanding. To play the summer game
Some owe their moms, beyond desire and time,
For ministrations gritty, not sublime.

Walter James Vincent "Rabbit" Maranville divided his illustrious career via sojourns in five National League cities, from 1912-34. He was inducted into Cooperstown in 1954.

June Ode

Some yards appear designed for whiffle ball.
A glassy grass plateau, with a short porch;
Young elms that overarch a picket wall
Form friendly confines wherein we can scorch
Or spray or swat or slam a plastic sphere
With bats that make us feel we swing the air.
Substantial lightness is, I think, that which
Impresses most on whiffle-ballers' minds:
The all-and-nothing hanging on each pitch—
A paradox enabling us to find
Brief respite via triumph or chagrin
From chasing balls that whiffle in the wind.

Tombeau d'Anton Bruckner

Binge listening to symphonies by Bruckner—
Past ten to zero he composed but one;
But what a one! Elevenfold, to stun
Imagination. Weary auditor
Elated by the escalating fanfares
That echo and re-echo in my ears,
I contemplate the simple man who turned
The orchestra into an organ; spurned
More than a modicum of variation
For the same singular exhilaration.

"The odd name for [Symphony Number zero] comes from an inscription by the composer on the title page. In 1895, when Bruckner reviewed his symphonies in order to have them published, he declared that this symphony 'does not count' (*'gilt nicht'*)."

–"Program Notes," MusicaNova
(author unidentified)

Of Intervals

Objective subjectivity of time.
Unlike the crash of waves on diverse days,
Each our minutes register the same—
And yet experientially amaze
By their disparity. Some moments
Barely measure their own transience.
Others threaten to outlast duration.
The chasm prompts our wonder. At creation
When the Timekeeper this paradox designed,
He limned the convolutions of man's mind.
.

Ll. 2-3: Cf. Shakespeare, *Sonnet 60*.

Homeric Hymn
(in re Springfield's EWS testing)

Inevitably come month's second Tuesday
Sirens sing—affair so regular
One's not so much attuned as that the ear
Their piercing wail fails to register.
Odysseus in town might even say,
"Who cares to hear their peal anyway?
Though I suppose those ladies serve a purpose
In the event of Scylla or Charybdis."

After Her Orchestration
(Homage to Corrine)

Champagne flutes glistening in the morning light
Toast the triumph of festivity last night.
At dinner parties, Dear, your *metier's*
The stuff of fiction: Mrs. Dalloway's
Soirees alone compare. Partakers *take parts*:
Briefly ennobled in your performance art.

Tafelmusik
(for Corrine)

Worcestershire (Heinz), bacon bits, and fine wine:
An eclectic assembly, favorites of mine,
Are prerequisite next to my plate when we dine;
Or at least preferential, though only the vine
 Proves essential—and to gaze in thine eyne.

Valentine

A quietude invests the winter cold
In compensation for the frigid winds
That narrate tacitly a tale told
At this time of the year since God knows when.
Blithe whisperings of vernal intimation
Encouraging our polar sublimation.
Spring soon, near silence sings. *Be still; be patient.*
Solicitude inveighs the wintry soul
Against indulging in her hermitage.
A score of days alone will take its toll
And stoke the embers of a smoldered rage.
Just as the short, dark days attain their end,
The sullen soul is lightened by a friend—
Or better, one's beloved; whence, we transcend.

Then

A night of intimacy like unto
Back when our souls embodied fused as one.
Back then. Deictics prove reflexive—*then*,
Then, augurs that past passionings of you
And I presage a renaissance of love.
As when a vessel long thought lost at sea
Surprisingly weighs anchor in the cove
From whence it sailed, so you return to me.

Epithalamion
(lauding twenty years)

Daunted by the day, bereft of words,
I sought sweet cues from inflections of the birds.
A cardinal on a pinnacle I passed
Appeared to chirrup, *true love ever lasts.*
A redbreast to the theme then leant her voice;
A blue jay medleyed that *all ought rejoice.*
The lark ascending (for you love that air)
Violaed sonorously to *prepare*
For festive recollections with dear friends.
Hence, here my anniversary lyric ends:
Let celebration of our vows commence.

Marconi in March

The wind shears play havoc with reception,
And I can fancy that Sebastian Bach
Is caught a bit by cumulus—a third
Of fugue or second part of an invention.
Who knows? Perhaps that circulating hawk
Or, drafting on the breeze, some other bird
Has caught upon the air the air we lost
When strains of the Baroque went tempest-tossed.

Gavotte

But a bit of the Baroque en route to Walgreens—
Unlikely I can state how much that means.
On runs (*pace* the pun) for sundry papers
Or some salve, Corelli's or Charpentier's
Refrains—though my missions forfeit measures—
Accord in fugues and chords augmenting pleasures:
A veritable trove of sonic treasures.
A harpsichordist somewhere in my brain
Completes their pieces over and again.

Aquarelle

The orange poppies in the mustard vase
 Divide the China chickens, who keep pace
With one another in an artifice
 Of pecking on the polished bureau. This
Tableaux is gilded by the morning sun.
And this water color sketch in verse is done.

Who Comes to Call No Cause for "Who Ya Gonna Call"

We puzzle at a crimson dresser drawer
Which, absent reason, every morn's ajar.
Perhaps the cats have pawed upon the knob—
But why? It's not a feline sort of job
So much as mischief by a poltergeist
In love with linen: too afraid to heist
Or toss the silks about the parlor floor.
Appeased by but a peek, and nothing more:
The napkin fetish of a ghost voyeur.

Spielberg among the Conifers

They re-ran *Close Encounters* yesternight—
And after massive synthesizer sounds,
And everywhere for Roy apparent mounds,
Uncannily the dark illumed a sight
Beyond the window of the giant pine
Truncated just so slightly at the crown—
Evoking fantasies of the returned
Eager to tell our world what they had learned.
So did conjunction of a film and tree
Fuel an alien reverie for me.

Statues on the Capitol Mall

The Monitor

The Dirksen mold resembles Christmas present.
Coyly couchant at his cast iron feet
Square off a donkey and an elephant—
Poised to devour, or at the least to beat
About the stately pantlegs of staid Dirksen,
Whose mien betrays mild boredom at these irksome
Partisans. Preoccupied, they fail to appear
Aware that they would tangle with a bear.

"My competitor in top of all design"
(*Antony and Cleopatra*, V.i.42)

Cast in bronze before the silver-domed State House,
The jowly, steely scowl of Stephen Douglas:
Protecting legislators from attack;
Ironically to Abe, *I've got your back*—
Since Douglas gazes at that taller monument
Of one who, in the flesh, kept just in front
Of him; although their first race ran the other's
Way. In lore, in fate, they link as brothers.

Memento

As though frozen by a Gorgon's head of flame
The firemen paradoxically repose
In stark activity. Two hoist a hose,
Another scales a ladder of the same
 Sort (although stone) we see on CNN
When such as they wage burning war again.
 Most days I pass the statue none are by;
 But this morning there appeared a family
Of four: the parents and a pair of boys
 Red-helmeted, with tonka trucks for toys,
Yet staid (who knows from where this quartet came?),
Combing the brick courtyard for a name.

Eternal Matinee
(*In Memory of Bob Melende*)

What makes a man check out at fifty-eight?
 Still single, Bo, perhaps you kept a date
With some late starlet of the silver screen:
 Kate Hepburn, Taylor, Davis, or Loren.
Your reservation of a booth for two
 I could forgive. Why choose to live when you
Could cast into a cinema surmise,
And stare forever into Greta Garbo's eyes.

That Day You Departed
(*In Memoriam, Myron Glazer*)

Winter thunder rarely rumbles here.
 Summer weather summons raucous storms.
 Even heavy snow falls silently.
 But death's a lifelong paradox: the harm
 Of respiration makes us disappear.
 No wonder, then, the skies roared violently—
 Casting in most apposite relief
 Our loss: your gentle soul and kindest life.

Measurements
(In Memory of B.P.)

A small thing ensuing from a tall:
A dangling branch, inches above my reach.
No stretch to garner in your grasp at all.
No reason to wrest it—yet if I could touch
It (so the magic cogitation runs)
From the dark wood you would reemerge at once.
In all the forest not another bough
Beyond me; solely in your compass, somehow…
Therefore, never to be twigged. I can but laugh
(Or cry). The world seems shorter by a half.

To Seventeen
(27 April 2019)

"Havlicek stole the ball!" croaked Johnny Most;
And with that call the kid became the toast
Of Beantown—blazed a trail for thieves to follow
(Or polished the parquet, we ought to say).
Hence, your departure renders somewhat hollow
Rites we've grown accustomed to in May
In part because of you. Still, we'll recall
At times when one in green purloins the ball.

Violincello

The radio lilts Mendelssohn three doors away—
And I can fancy, I can hope and pray
That you perform him in some distant room:
Which begs the question, Rachel, play for whom?

The young composer, like you, left too soon.
His dateless night, like yours, arrived at noon.
And since he lost a sister, just as I
For you have on occasion cause to cry,
I like to think you bow the vocalise
For him, another brother you can please.

"dateless night": Cf. Shakespeare *Sonnet 30.6*.

Memorial

Red appears the color of this day
Commencing summer. Elegant elderly
Ladies in scarlet greet me on my walk.
My neighbor's carmine yacht's unmoored from dry dock.
The slight breeze troubling the flags unfurled
Picks up so that the stripes round poles are curled
As though for barbershops: white-rapt-in-red.
So many flags, recalling all our dead,
In featured color of the blood they shed.
No summertime, no other time instead.

NATURA NATURANS

Look down and find configurations of the clouds
Caught in puddles imitating ponds
That could accommodate unwitting swans.
The Torrents of Spring *for Hemingway were owed*
To mocking Sherwood Anderson's effusions.
No novelist's needed to limn ***these*** *profusions*
Concatenating on the cobbled roof—
Though poets from a storm are not aloof,
Of course. We're cued from Nature's trope commands
To make from her: ***Natura Naturans****.*

Natura naturans (Lat.): **Nature naturing**—*her self-actualization; in conjunction, the poet may be construed in terms of* **natura naturata**, *a receptor of "whatever follows from the necessity of [***natura naturans***]" (Spinoza,* **Ethics** *[1677]). Cf.* **The Winter's Tale**, *IV.iv.87:*

> There is an art which in [its] piedness shares
> With great creating Nature…
> Yet Nature is made better by no mean
> But Nature makes that mean: so over that art
> Which…adds to Nature, is an art
> That Nature makes.

"You do not **copy** nature—you make something which is an **imitation** of nature—read your Aristotle again. That is the **work** of the imagination, as the late Virginia Woolf pointed out. You have to work, you have to imagine… Arrived at that condition, the imagination inflamed, the excitement of it is that you…become the instrument of nature.…by housing a spirit, as nature houses juice in an apple.
—William Carlos Williams

Ll. 1–2: Cf. Alexander Pope, **Windsor Forest** (1713):

> Oft in her Glass the musing shepherd spies
> The headlong Mountains and the downward Skies,

The Torrents of Spring, A Romantic Novel in Honor of the Passing of a Great Race (1926), Hemingway's first work of any length, parodies Sherwood Anderson's **Dark Laughter** (1925). Hadley Richardson, then married to Hemingway, thought the portraiture of O'Neill (based on Anderson) "nasty"; and Gertrude Stein "fell out" with the young Turk over his callous spoofing of a mentor.

Shouldering the Weather

Chicago cold seems unlike any other.
The whipping winds, of course, but something more
Abets unique frigidity: décor.
Lake Michigan along the Mile blues
Its semi-frozen floes; and one construes
The Sears Tower a black obelisk of ice.
Even Navy Pier and Wrigley bother
In December as incongruous,
For they belong to summer festival.
Chicago Augusts prove nonpareil.

Discretion Is

Suburban stalactites depend from Durkee's roof,
Endangering the field mice enough
To pass on the propitiatory cheese
And on their own recognizance keep out
From underneath the door. Icicles raise doubt:
Better safe than skewered by deep freeze.

Snolykta
(for Joanne Durkee)

Snolykta! Paradoxic pyramid
Of Isoscelic ice encasing flame.
Mysterious invention Sweden would
Aspire anachronistically to claim
A share of fame with ancient Egypt. Sands
Are sun-baked. But in distant northern lands
Material is polished from inside
A frozen hollow. Architects deride
The logical and scientific dicta
To erect the arctic miracle of *snolykta*.

"Nel foco che li affina"
(*Purgatorio, XXVI.148*)

The pyramid of snow is lit within;
Its stacked orbs beacon frozen paradox.
The flame concealed burnishes; it licks
Yet hardens walls of ice. When we again
Must venture forth in temperatures below,
Recall the core that's steeled by the glow.

Reprieve

The dregs of winter cannot but depress.
When one peers out the window or the door,
A speckled gray and tawny sordidness
 Pervades the *inward* nature to the core.
Yet should a cardinal flit across the pane,
 Its splash of red reflects upon the soul.
That pigment tincture registered therein
Abates the gloom. Though season take its toll,
 Reminders that the scene proves temporary
Can mitigate the dearth of February.

Vernal Prelude
(*20 February*)

Gelid droplets masquerade as buds
On a soggier than icy afternoon.
One happily acknowledges the mud's
 Veneer as prelude to the garden beds
Of April predicating blooms in June—
And swinging V's of the returning birds
 Evoke these imitative beads of words.
The stinging winds still whisper *Springtime soon*.

Garden Harbinger

The thaw lends an impress of seedbeds of snow,
 Replacing boxed flowers of six months ago,
And various vegetables, each to its row.

With more warmth the white crop shall quickly have gone,
The reaping by virtue of late winter sun;
A transient prelude of sowing to come.

March

Came in neither like lion nor like lamb,
But as the possums nosing round at night:
Fierce yet skittish, mottled grey and white.
In search of sustenance, they waddle from
Wherever they have lain through winter days;
Heads soaked by sipping in the water bowl,
Wide-eyed and teething a bewildered scowl,
An animalization of malaise.
Yet when one ferrets near the garden fence,
It intimates that April hails hence.

Fair Fowl Weather

A veritable flurry of Snow Geese
Cascades upon the Central Kansas plain.
A sudden shower of winged white; they cease,
Briefly, their flight in search of remnant grain,
Their journey further northward to sustain.
At once, a wonder: Snow falls *up* in air!
The gaggle storm shall strike again somewhere
Between the Manitoban steppes and here.

Medleyed

With complex crisscross undulating V's
 Blue sky is scored by hordes of Canadian Geese—
Whose honking, high reverberant stark sound
Concatenates a monotonic round
As consort to the interactive vectors
That seem in turn to portion tone in sectors.

Geometry and jocund din together
Are more than figurative birds of feather.

L. 7. Cf. Wordsworth, "There Was a Boy," the owls' "concourse wild Of jocund din."

Paired in the Palette of March

The cardinals pecking at the sweet-elm flowers
Comprise a carmine medley: red on red.
The jays that meld with sky in daytime hours
Suggest a congeries of blue instead.
The grass, and verdant ferns that grace the vase
Conjecture green ought garner pride of place.
Chess pieces tinctured by the alcove light
Append a modest tone of black and white.

Cat at the Window

Feline peeking out upon March first.
Winter still might summon up its worst
For twenty days or so—but Kitty knows
Late white precipitation, final snows
Are but that. Her excitement broaches words
But purrs shall have to mime, *Bring on the birds!*
Those mornings padding to the door in hope
That it would open onto Spring, with *Nope*
The portal's adamant reply, are over.
Count down the hours 'till Kitty rolls in clover.

Cat and Cactus

Her scrutiny of all its tiny claws
Evokes a nascent fear, which proves the cause
Of wary hesitation; gives her pause,
Discouraging light batting with her paws.
Its prickly mien betokens truculence.
On prowls she's not encountered succulents.
Hence, thinks (perhaps) 'tis better to ignore,
Turns tail, and pads elsewhere to explore.

Bast

Plush on the cushions the white puss reclines.
Her kitten eyes betray experience.
Not nine lives but nine thousand prowled since
She moused the rodents round Egyptian mines.
*Way back when soothsayers accorded felines
Proper due*, perhaps puss meditates.
Though only a Nakata could translate
Her purrs. And plausibly she's no designs
Other than to laze out on the cushions;
All times perpetually now in her devotions.

Bast: Ancient Egyptian cat deity.

Nakata: Character in Haruki Murakami's *Kafka on the Shore* who can converse with cats.

From Her Bird Seat

In days of yore a cat stuck in a tree
Was rescued by the volunteer FD.
Apparently, that epoch's past. And cats
Require heroes who don other hats:
A specialist on trees, your next door neighbor;
An enterprising kid, for feline labor—
Or a hungry squirrel on a nearby branch
With *turnabout fair play* regarding lunch.
The rodent need be large, the cat a kitten
For the prospect to prove real of being eaten,
Or at the least, severely chewed and bitten.
Betwixt two frights, the puss might well descend
Upon her own. Shake tail at tale's end.

Crochat

Instinct apodictic—for how could Kitty *learn*
To so engross herself with a ball of yarn?
Yet every strand of scarf you try to knit
Unravels as she claws the source of it;
Whereas my lines our puss could claim to purl,
Deriving from a playful, purring girl.

Cupidi(kit)ty

Our cats attach themselves to household things.
Miss Margo has *her* lamp; Henry *his* bowl:
Familiar thrill of ownership that brings
Materialist comfort to the soul.
To witness which disturbs somewhat, for that's
Reflective of our feelings toward *our* cats.

Tandem Nap

Cat at my elbow. Margueritte, my love:
Sweetheart, Honey, Kitty-pie; above
All other felines purring 'neath the moon
My choice with whom to dream of runcible spoon.

Cf. Edward Lear, "The Owl and the Pussy-Cat."

Corollae

Instanter the pink magnolias popped;
And overnight star sisters followed suit
In white, declaring winter woes had stopped—
Albeit northern snowfall, rendered moot
By implacable desire to will in Spring,
Confirmed by the magnolias blossoming.

Spring Chiaroscuro
(for Peter Shapinsky)

Late April morning skies loom overcast,
And branches get entangled in the gloom.
So close the atmosphere, there seems no room
To bloom; but redbuds manage, and are cast
Against the dark in stark violet relief.
Irradiance astonishingly brief;
Rays storm the clouds, and shred the haze in shards,
The sun her gray dishabille discards.

A Momentary Petal Dispensation

The dominance of tulips on my walk
Ravishes the eye. The carmine, golden, pied,
Pure white, alone or clustered, seem allied
In colonizing Hawthorne Place. All squawk
Of realpolitik and worldly powers
Is silenced by the placid reign of flowers.

Cf. Frost: "The figure a poem makes" comprises "a momentary stay against confusion."

Mnemonic

Strewn pedals on the sidewalks signal soon
Enough that pink and white will cede to green
As May gives way to darker hues of June.
My mood on morning strolls, mostly serene,
Is counterpointed slightly, for the season's
Transformations recollect the temporal treasons
That poach a pence from life's purse every day,
And caveat against a lengthier stay.

Viola Tricolor Tough Guy

An etymological mystery to me,
The slander of pusillanimity toward the pansy.
A hardier flower proves difficult to find—
Why, then, are pansies so heedlessly maligned?
A caveat opposing ignorance, they
 Fuel as fillip this peculiar pensée.

Augury

Salvia regina spire purple praise,
That the sun queen might espy their silent song.
Although perennials, not lasting long:
Ultimately battered by the torrid days.
Yet salvias' transience breeds longevity—
They wilt that in descendants they return;
Like our own generational activity
Unless (until?) we scorch the earth and burn.
Pathetic fallacy encoding warning
Of the pathos apropos to global warming.

Trumpet Vines

Musically misnamed, they compare more to trombones,
Or to elaborate horns of gramophones.
In either case, their twining round our garden
Recalls Grandpa's recordings of Teagarden.
The mind's ear fancies through their elegance
Muted solos counterpointing silence,
While in the wind the nearby harebells dance.

Not Much Ado, yet Something

Verbenas waft supremely when I pass,
Their fragrance reminiscent of a lass.
'Tis just as Dogberry told us:
Comparison proves od'rous.
Sagacity from a self-insistent ass.

Cf. *Much Ado about Nothing*, III.v.15; IV.ii.79.

Spelled with a Y

The peonies synaesthetically perform
Through pink proliferations of perfume.
An odored, colored dance that might alarm
The hyper-sensitive, but does no harm—
Unless disturbing puritans, perhaps,
Who ken from sensuous allure our lapse;
Forgetting Eden *planted as a garden*
By One from Whom those puritans beg pardon.
In retrospect, one finds it sadly odd
How frightened Evangelicals damn God.

Potted Panopticon

Argus eyed and right outside my door,
The white-pink vinca stare me into day.
No time to pause and count, though still I'd say
In number they approximate a score.
And now regardless of what ways I take,
I'm haunted in their horticultured wake.

My acts and reticences miles from here,
What all I pounce upon or do not dare
Commit to out of ignorance or fear,
And consequently wish would disappear
So that I might dismiss things from my care
Are frozen by that particolored stare—
Which to my mind surveils everywhere.

Yet as happens that mere chance impression
Can predicate ridiculous obsession,
Conceding such, I'll liberate my hours
From the unwitting tyranny of flowers.

Tractatus Hydrangeas

Can Wittgenstein apply to the hydrangeas?
When seen aright, most things are understood.
Hydrangeas ornament most every house
In the circumference of our neighborhood.
Yet ultimately what is there to know
About our friends' proclivity to grow
Bine stems that parachute in white and pink,
And only for a poem's sake make one think?
Herr Doktor also taught that mere description
Ought override explanatory fiction.

Edeladweiss, or Fleur-de-lycee

Lilacs that fester still smell rather well;
Hence to dispense with them we felt no urge.
No base infection prompted they be purged;
Although they wilted, wafted—what the hell.
Having no power to hurt, in any case,
Completely innocent, no *fleurs du mal*.
Evil to lilacs means nothing at all,
Nor to their fellows of the floral race.
Yet many a man who sports a boutonière,
Dandiness notwithstanding, mongers fear.
Would that men culled a lesson from the flowers
And cultivated aromatic powers.
Then, though no gods, since man but proposes,
More would manifest as daffodils and roses.
.

Lilacs: Cf. Shakespeare *Sonnet 94*

Not Always

Catalpa trees birds favor for their shelter,
And caterpillars feast upon their leaves.
Deciduous, they shade from summer swelter.
Their roots in winter roil some from frost heaves.
The facet of Catalpas that's bizarre
Consists in alter-sobriquet: *Cigar*.
Etymologically, they render void
A quaint surmise by Dr. Sigmund Freud.

Elevenish Caprice

The mimesis of mimosas appertains
To actuality. In wind, they're fans.
Their drink deceives, though, inasmuch as fronds
Are merely imitated by the champagne's
Orange tincture. As for taste, the tree
Defies an effervesced analogy.—
Likening's limit's instanced by a branch
In conjunction with its namesake of a brunch.

Obcidatus

The tree though not its mulberries I'll miss;
Its messy mash begrimes the ground iwis.
Though in majestic imitation of
Yggdrasil entangling fiery cars above,
Or of the trunk of knowledge in the Garden,
Which plucked of fruit denied our Parents pardon,
The mulberry still fell victim to the saw.
Its detritus shall disappear by law
Of natural cessation. Hence, next Spring
The ground, though clean, shall seem a lesser thing.

Etiolate

All up the route the startled motorist sees
The fatal irony of bare ash trees.
Due to the bores, they died down to their names.
Better, perhaps, to have been swallowed in flames.
Same nominal twist and pathetic story,
Though no remnants remaining to look so sorry
And cast in relief their former emerald glory.
Not that they stood out prominently then,
But with arboreal brethren blended in.

We seek in all surroundings symmetries
And resonances, continuities.
It stings—we can't restore such to these trees.

Southwestern Sojourn

Arizonan flora balks the mind:
The cacti, Palo Verde, sage and palms
  Refuse a poet's likening in kind.
They *are*; apt subjects in themselves for psalms.

'Zonan fauna, on the other hand—
  Roadrunner shredding torrid desert lane,
  Coyote keening like a lass in pain,
  Hawk in high hermitage—figure this land,

The lay of which inspires another hymn,
As mesas shoulder sky in metonym.

Train

Coyotes, I am told, first feed their weak
And elderly and young; assist their sick
Before they satisfy themselves with spoil.
Instinctively, their predatory toil
Is predicated on the health of whole.
Coyotes as a pack possess a soul.
On chill, desert nights, they keen, we shudder.
But they kill for care; we merely murder.

Sunny Morning at Sonoma Estates

Lemon-lamps adorn their namesake trees,
And palms form stanchions steadying the sky.
Cacti prick resistant in the breeze,
And Palo Verde hang the air with green.
Even the yellow fire hydrants try
To blend with the suburban desert scene.
Some bungalows along the walks
Are fronted by large variegated rocks.
Sprinkles puddle on the artificial grass
(One reason why our water mightn't last).

Under Sun Instead of Glass
(or The Fat Quacks of Phoenix)

PLEASE DON'T FEED THE DUCKS, the placard reads.
I understand. Slick plumage hardly needs
More scraps to swell already burly pelts.
One can't in conscience call these mallards svelte,
Beyond large wigeon shadows of a doubt.
They waddle round the golf course pond; so stout,
Such billed rotundities with webbed feet
Stir restauranter dreams of duck confit.

Urban Avian

Bird on a hydrant rather than a wire,
Forced to fly in the event of fire—
As apotheosis, or to simply flee:
Are you the phoenix or a chickadee?

Vulgivagus Cavia Porcellus

Fluffy for sale? No, Fluffy for *free*!
The six-year old next door's menagerie,
Replete with cats, canaries, and a dog,
Cannot comprise a small, domestic hog.
They tried. He brought back Fluff from Show and Tell,
Dispensed with by another kid pell mell,
Whose mom instructed, *bring the beast to school.*
Perhaps a friend might like the nibbling fool
(*And take that goddamn guinea off our hands;*
To feed, and clean the pen's not in my plans.)
Small histories repeat; and thus, with Fluff.
The neighbor child's parent said *enough*.
(Itinerant rodents truly have it rough.)
Hence, where to next? His furry jowls appeal—
Yet should Kitty trick the cage, then Fluff's a meal.

Hare Brain

I shan't pretend to know the mind of rabbits,
Nor venture whether they possess a mind.
Yet from convention of prosodic habits—
On walks, from chance encounters with their kind,
I might surmise they don't desire much:
Some blades to nibble, water, and a hutch;
For such, no competition from a rat;
And absence of the predatory cat.
(Perhaps, when Peter sleeps a carrot seems
The veritable vegetable of dreams.)

Parvum Addendum

They would assert themselves despite concrete:
The blades discovering between the squares
A cranny to emerge from and declare
As colony to lawn that lines the street.
Cricket its viceroy, tyrant of the turf,
And overlord of lowly insect surf.
Though study; *scrutinize*—you may discern
Resistance in the weeds: the worm shall turn.
Minutiae moralized by Ezra Pound:
The ant's a centaur in his world—pull down!

Cf. Pound, *Canto LXXXI*: "The ant's a centaur in his dragon world. / Pull down thy vanity, it is not man / Made courage, or made order, or made grace, / Pull down thy vanity, I say pull down."

Adagio

The Monarch hide-and-seeking in the bush,
Does it divine that soon its wings will close
Forever? Supposedly, alone man knows
Life's sought cacophony shall someday hush.
Alone. Though knowledge may be preached to choir,
The final song's sung solo—news as dire.
Duet of fatal facts. Music that haunts
Our steps in tempo to the daunting dance.

Two Montpelier Portraits

Zenith

Where do mountains end and clouds commence?
Grey-blue configurations are so dense
In these environs, one might think, up here,
As ground ascends it tapers into air
And in the thither realm of atmosphere
Does not so much as peak as disappear.
Where would I wind up if I could mount
Horizon's escalator up Vermont?

Aletheia

On certain days from out the clouds mounts rise,
As though discarding cumulus disguise;
Assert themselves against the air, terrain
Between the blues of sky and Lake Champlain,
And, further testifying *We are here*,
The peaks inscribe their craggy signature—
Impress their Hancock in a forest font
Upon the greenwood foolscap of Vermont.

Tornado Watch

The wind not only swept, but polished stars—
Or so it seemed; and wooded city streets.
The boughs of elms and oaks rained down in sheets,
Hence threatened stray pedestrians, and cars.
But who'd not walk about or drive to spy
Above the plains the diamonds in the sky?
Phenomenal treasure trove of wind, stars, night:
Dazzling, ravishing, transfixing sight!

Savannahs

What is it that accounts for open fields
 Unlocking all emotion? Reason yields
To seas of soy or corn, to cultivated green
 Of golf or diamonds: any vista seen
That situates the stars before my eyes
 As well as overhead; that shall apprise
 Of lightning storms that on flat platforms dance
And signal strollers of their hairbreadth chance,
 By hastening home, to outrace inundation.
 For me, horizons constitute foundations.
Though I marvel at the majesty of mountains;
 Likewise, revere the violent torque of fountains
 Sheering down from cliffs to detonate—
From early on in my novitiate
To nature, heart and soul were pledged to plains.
The beatific horizontal reigns.

N.N.
(*reprise*)

The rain in its own laving way wilts flowers.
The searing sun does not monopolize
Those means by which the cowslips meet demise,
And tulips lose their scintillating power.
Then, too, seasonal attrition at this hour
Of summer's waning day disturbs my eyes,
Knowledge of Nature's nature notwithstanding.
But why object? She's deaf to reprimanding.
So sun and rain and time will have their way,
And Nature's own by Nature be stolen away.

Four Seasons

The sky's pieced out with robin's egg blue squares—
Mid August, though there's autumn in the air;
And cloud wisps scudding South anticipate
The snowbirds in late equinoctial flight
To temperate climes—'til constellations bring
Them word of Northern warmth, and herald Spring.

Sennet

The season changed along with owl's call
  Like unto none heard heretofore at all:
A garbled, trisyllabic *hoo-hoo-haw*
As though the nibbled moon caught in its craw.
The night owl's autumnal indigestion
  Broaching with browning leaves September question,
Is this an equinox that isn't right,
A Fall presaging falls? Or is my fright
A misbegotten chimera, brought about
  By a cold wind and a disarming hoot?

"A nameless air"

Albino pumpkin plump against the wall:
Live placard for first festival of Fall,
Announcing Hallow's Eve in bulbous white.
The hunter's moon, instead, lends orange light.

Two autumn lamps, adorning sky and sill
In transient splendor—only gleaming till
The one's extinguished at the break of day,
The other to be tossed before decay.

Short shrift discerned in any form seems sober,
But somehow more so (why?) in mid-October.

Title: Cf. Wallace Stevens, "Autumn Refrain."

Autumn Denouement

Today dry stalks resemble their faux sentries,
Men of straw devised to frighten crows.
And withered tassels rattle in a breeze
That, notwithstanding slight, lays out in rows
Sere sheaves, and scatters kernels for the mice
Who glean a harvest of their own. Suffice
To say this round of sow and reap near done.
The denouement of autumn has begun.

Thaw Thought

Nothing but a brief reprieve, I know.
Still, though, evaporating early snow
Post premature precipitation lifts
Fond fantasy. Number among November's gifts
Even unfounded hope. Late Indian summer
Dreams warm imagination's winter slumber—
Slightly offsetting the waking cold bummer.

Entomologous

The bug climbs skyward on extended pedes;
The windowpane provides the warmth he needs.
His brothers in the basement tap the dryer
That combusts within perpetuating fire
Sufficient as the pane proves for the flier.
Survival in December is a dire
Contest insects must inevitably lose:
They caveat for creatures who can choose.

Dome

Dear God, the stars seem polished on this night!
Embedded in the velvet blue, their white
Minute and scintillant appearance
Amounts to planets of circumference,
For all they imitate Aquinas pins
On which the angels dance to pardon sins.

Or if that fancy strains credulity,
Then to the best of my ability
I'll reconceive a white infinitude
Behind the blue veneer, with light exud-
ing through designed celestial holes
To glimmer nightly hope for lonely souls.

White in blue, or blue disclosing white:
Divine chiaroscuro dazzles sight.

The Rain Reminds Me

I ought have caught an inkling when a *hose*
Entangled my initial steps to town.
Albeit it sprinkling I did not suppose
Torrential sheets would *instanter* rain down
And unsuspecting rats and field mice drown.
Although for me not fatal, the flash flood
Recalled our shared mammalian brotherhood,
And recollected I, like they, soaked here
Because an Elder gathered up in pairs
All species rescued from diluvian biers.

Many Beds in His Garden

An amarilliant sheen of dandelions
 Extending near as far my eye can see:
 In splendid horticultural alliance
With scrub oaks arborists begrudge as trees.
 But assume the Architect of Nature's needs
And come a cropper. *God sows no weeds.*

HOMAGE THROUGH HOPKINS AND HERBERT

The world is charged with the grandeur of God.
Let me not love Thee if I love Thee not.

Circumambient

Under the early Sunday traffic comes
The Grace Church organist piping hymns;
And in the whistle of the locomotive
One imagines a soprano by the votive
Candles, in imitation, via voice,
Of amber flickers signaling *rejoice!*
In color comparable to caution lights
That slow those cars the organist delights
To murmur under. Nothing exceeds the compass
Of Holiness; outside resides inside of Grace.

Installations

The prints of sun upon the parquet floor
 Form superimpositions of the squares
That carpenters ingrained decades before.
And outside likewise shades of clouds appear
As products of diaphanous design.
The light by which we see is God's own sign
As well—Whose masterworks in miniature
Amalgamate His art and signature.

A Chapel in Santa Fe

The stairway of Loretto has no known source,
 Unless indeed elicited by prayer.
One day a carpenter arrived on horse.
 He built the stairs and vanished in thin air.
The nuns novenad Joseph in their plight,
 Yet is it so unlikely that they might
 Have ascertained a still ulterior height?
One facet of the structure stuns the mind:
Absence of any nails implies Divine
Apprentice work. The Lord absorbed before
The bolts. Perhaps He kept that plan in store.

Laudatus Two
(17 March)

Out of Ireland Saint Patrick drove the snakes
In sacred antithetical relation:
The slitherers must exit for salvation.
Yet hagiographers, for Gertrude's sake,
Remind that other creatures we embrace
This day: the whiskered, furry feline race
To whom she ministered, and harbored haven.
Strong argument that cats shall enter heaven.

Notre Dame

This April morn the steeples in our city
Still as always punctuate the sky.
Impossible that spires recede in pity,
Impossible that architraves should cry.
Concatenated chimes still herald the hour
In syncopation—bells split seconds apart.
The sun through stained glass rains a color shower;
At noon the organ concerts will still start.
Though Bach and Handel move the listener's heart,
Music today affords no sanctuary.
The chimes, the spires, the glass from mind depart,
And anomie attacks the soul. We're weary
From the Paris fires that raged throughout the night
In stark antithesis to Holy Light.

Might

Yet then again, yes, *then again*, *good* God—
Albeit an act horrifically odd
As dire reminder of His omnipresent
 Love—just might resort to complex precedent.
This time of year recalls the bush that burned,
The Son He sacrificed for us returned.
Torrents dousing the Cathedral flames had so
To scour the skies they might have left a rainbow;
Though gaping in the dark, we could not see.
 Call these Rose-colored thoughts—they might well be.
Yet as through holy glass sun tinctures light,
Affirming faith, might God fix inward sight.

Kafka's Psalm
(Turned to verse, from Gershom Scholem)

Are we absent any access in deep night
From your breath of peace—asphyxiated quite?

Can your Absolute have absolutely died
In the void of Zion—never here descried

Where the medium of life is mere deception,
Incapable of harboring Conception?

Grant, God, man pierced by the power of your Nil,
Such that Nothingness eviscerates our ill.

Matthew 10:29

The providence inferred from fall of sparrow
Is hard to countenance. For why ought sorrow
Guarantee a kinder dispensation?
How rarely suited to our situation
Proves the optimistic gist of words
That garner solace from the death of birds.

Today that saying, like a verbal poultice,
Seems noxiously so skewed as to revolt us.
But then, if Christ (and Hamlet) mouth it,
We might—at *times*—think twice before we doubt it.

Cf. *Hamlet*, V.ii.233.

Transport

NO SKATEBOARDING ON CHURCH PROPERTY. Okay.
Suppose some wispy, bearded, boarding youth
Rolled up the wheelchair ramp proclaiming Truth?
Intrigued by his word that he might be the Way,
Would his means of convoy your conviction sway,
And would you to cops the kid (the Christ?) betray?
(A la the Grand Inquisitor who dismissed Him—
Upon which our savior up and kissed him.)
When the Second Coming finally comes to pass,
Perhaps the skateboard shall replace the ass.

Summa contra Gentiles

A house of worship in desuetude
 Has ceded to a creed less crass than crude.
Another *Cross*(*Fit Inc.*) is there installed
That might erstwhile parishioners appall
Were any 'round. They've gone the way of winds.
A gym replacing church redresses sins.
The out-of-shape, instead of seeking God,
 Make pilgrimage to *CrossFit* for their WOD,
 In raptures risking ruptures—sacrifice
To "Holy Trinity of Exercise."
 Don't, please, misapprehend: fitness is fine.
We err, though, in mistaking it Divine.

Ll. 1-3: The former Fifth Street Evangelical Chapel in Springfield, IL., was bought and remodeled by the conditioning franchise.

Ll. 8-10: The high intensity WORKOUT OF THE DAY, lauded in a CrossFit video as "the Holy Trinity of Exercise," has been criticized for augmenting risk of exertional rhabdomyolisis.

Paying Forward
(*Paradise Lost, III.341*)

By substitution of a single word
The gesture, just the same, is redirected:
A finer recompense by paying forward,
Augmenting wider fellowship affected.
The man to whom today I gave the five
Remarked he'd pass it on. Help him survive,
He'll aid a brother. Economics to exist!
The cause for all, would all were to enlist,
Would resurrect as everyone the Christ.

Noel 2019

Hodie Christus natus est, the tense
Betrays the challenge, dooming common sense.
Present *is* past *perfect* in more ways than one
When we contemplate our fate under the Son.
Birth—and death—at one and for all time:
Transcendent unity symbolized by rhyme,
For every moment is identified
In Divine paradox: we live because He died.

(*Goddamn*

Two thousand and twenty years—or so.
Nativity. The Prince of Peace. Although
For Christ's sake the wars waged 'twixt "Us" and "Them"
Number more than the years ago from Bethlehem.
Even internecine: **vide** *Reformation.*
The toll is obscene. The roll of annihilation
In the wake of the blessed Babe runs too long to read.
Bloody irony: He manifests our need.)

TRAGICOMIC ENTR'ACTE

Airport Prayer

The tendrils of the Sears Tower nearly reach
The plane, or so it seems. And at O'Hare
Young parents swing their child in the air.
In transit. Holy Father, you can teach
(Omnipotence is such) a loving son
Who rages 'gainst the dying of the light,
The means to deal with consuming fright
In the event his father's days are done.
Yet let the mortal spirit best the letter:
Please, Lord, permit Mike Lewis to get better.

Michael and Martha (and Me)

What to give one who ("literally") saved his life
"Three times at least," though "she'll not take from me
A thing that costs a dime," since bankruptcy
Confounds him, with illness abetting strife.
And the woman he desires as his wife
In these last chapters of his history—
She loves him, but not *thus*—augments his misery
Through no fault of her own. A fond belief
In change of heart resuscitates. Again,
Ironically this time, she rescues him.
Love that preserves is often wrought with pain.
His son, assessing circumstance, can't claim
More comprehension; blesses any means
That keep Dad dreaming; and thanks God that Dad dreams.

Seventh Stage

It is what it is, and *what* it is, is sad.
Decrepitude is wisdom? Yeats was mad.
Could we but stop the clock, shout *No* to change;
Or at the least, the last years rearrange,
Or beg an amnesty from ills of age,
And just grow older simply, pain assuage
(And *pace Conscious impotence of rage*).
My parents, dying—Lord, succor them for me:
Suffer thy elder children unto Thee.

Title: Cf. *As You Like It*, II.vii.170ff.
L. 2: Cf. "After Long Silence," l. 7.
L. 7: Cf. Eliot, "Little Gidding," II.
L. 9: Cf. Matthew, 19:14.

Mutatis Mutandis

Mutatis mutandis: what once was reversed.
The Latin for *inevitably cursed*.
The father who indoctrinates his son
Is subject to son's rule when day's near done.
The mother nursing babe with tender breast,
Untethered by dementia, strained, depressed
In final years, is nursed herself at home
She does not know, where son and daughter come
With kids in tow, once every month (or so)
To visit, kiss her puzzled face, and go
In guilt and shame—haunted by circumstances
Rotten as wrought: *mutatis mutandis*.

Blank Study

In the dim dementia of her life's December
At a window in a Newton nursing home
My mother stares. What does she still remember?
What images precipitate her calm
Or agitation, a smile or a tear?
She knows me yet—yet shall I disappear?

"Well Done, Thou Good and Faithful Servant"

Not to ponder too pathetically—
Today when we detached the Christmas tree
From its watered mooring, unlatched the balls,
Repealed its winter sublet in the hall,
And dragged the bedraggled conifer to the curb—
It needed doing, still the task disturbed.
I'd like to think somewhere a sacred wood
Keeps evergreen those needled that had stood.

The Collector
(*for Cheryl Pence*)

Griggsville, Sheffield, Sheldon. Can one find
A Carnegie postcard to appease the mind?
The sedulous librarian (retired)
Persists in her quest to ascertain the rest
Of those austere daguerreotypes inspired
By the habitations of our tomes that best
Make manifest humanity's potential
To literally *come to terms*: essential.

Homage to Nicolas Jenson (and Mark Pence)

Essis ad maloriat,
Ut vero core dolore.
The Nueva minions scroll their loony way.
Os niat venibh elsissi
Et loriyat praesentnit,
Typed cyphers spelling out absurdity.
Equat sequamet aliquam
Dolor odisprud duex.
To predicate the finest format style
Lis augiat nim il ulla
Consequate enit mod tat
We fool some with faux Latin for a while.

Nicolas Jenson (1420-1480), French engraver, pioneer printer and type designer—justly iconic to contemporary savants of the formatting art—like the other gentleman commended here.

To Carol Twombly, who devised the Nueva font, the poet's apologies for failing to acknowledge *in* these lines.

HARVARD VERSES

Composed in Harvard Yard
(5 July, 2019)

Ve*ri*tas, though parsed in three, remains the truth.
Through syll*a*bi*fi*ca*tion one can see
That, schism notwithstanding, unity
Prevails. *Amor* halved can neither salve nor soothe,
And Latin *Pax* is haunted by *Romanus*.
But the steely grip of *Veritas* upon us,
Ineluctably ingrained in us,
Conditions correspondence we can trust.
Peace and love we seek; the truth's a must.

Pine in the Sand

What can be garnered from a pine tree in the sand
 Apparently affixed to measure change?
The whims of Cambridge weather rearrange
 In random dispensations—oddly, planned:
 Vicissitude's the order of the day
When art *intends* that chance should have its way.
As Nietzschean philosophy distills,
 Fortune turns to chance through he who wills.
Yet grains of sand, since also grains of time,
 Imply another marker as the pine;
An intimation of the final change
 One hopes, yet doubts, proves *something rich and strange.*

Title: Moniker of Installation in front of Harvard Office of Admissions.
L. 12: Cf. *The Tempest*, I.ii.399.

Back Then Again

Cato and Neptune are buried in this ground
With white men who too felt the mortal wound,
Yet took a bullet or a bayonet
For cause that would reward them had not fate
Otherwise arbitred. But the pair of slaves,
Their names barely discernible on graves
In ancient Cambridge Cemetery, paid
For what would never have been theirs. A plaque
Commemorating them that's there displayed
Inscribes inequity for simply being black.

A Lob's Length from the Lab

They are batting tennis balls by Astrophysics.
The *mise en scene* seems most appropriate
For modern Niels Bohrs, Alberts, and Sir Isaacs—
Mens sano in corpore…, and all that.
Moreover, rubber orb trajectories
Ought surely arithmetic mind-sets please.
Or then again, in recreation parks
These physicists might seek release from quarks.

Chiseled Motto Addendum

"Non sub Homine sed sub Deo Lege,"
  Sed sub Deo Gracias etiam:
  Parallel pillars in the identity
  Of One *pro homine* I am that I am.
  To Langdell Hall's append this *aliud*,
  For God's not only great but also good.

Christened after Harvard Law School Dean Charles C. Langdell, Langdell Hall houses the largest academic legal library in the world.

On the Waters

Rowing in the rain. The element returns
In kind, in droplets, what the paddle churns:
Showers for strokes. Both beat upon the Charles,
The storm and sculler; but they're harmless churls.
There's no disturbing that which cannot care;
No troubling a body unaware.

Coterie Redux

Cambridge at any time is full of ghosts,
Ralph Waldo wrote. Does his own shade, august,
Hover round the Hall named after him?
Or does he saunter, on a transcendental whim,
Across the Yard locked arm-in-arm with Howells
En route to tea and cake at Russell Lowell's;
Or for cider (stronger fare) at Harvard Pub
Where H.D. Thoreau scribbles to their nub
The pencils that accounted for Pa's pelf,
And backed his civilly disobedient self?
With Hank and Billy James they raise a toast
To past as present: Cambridge full of ghosts.

John Thoreau, Sr. (1787-1859) owned a pencil factory in Concord, MA.

BUT SOMETIMES THE SNIDE'S ON YOU:
Poems Peevish

Unrequited

In the spirit of Auden, Larkin, and Wendy Cope,
Your poets with whom this author would humbly align,
A manuscript I submit—harboring hope
(However slight) that Faber editors find
It worthy of publication—for grace of line,
Dry wit, subtle passion, and nuanced jest
From across the pond. For the public? You'll judge best.

Far Better Fared So
(*on not contracting with a particular press*)

Since Publication—is indeed an Auction,
My letter to the World will have to wait.
As pay to print—for me—proves Not an Option:
Chagrin and Pride would ceaselessly debate
Over the tenor of the Referee—
Swayed by talent—or my vanity.

The wider Realm thus mightn't write of me.
Though I'll survive confined—in Coterie—
To unseen Hands this verse shall never pass
Demeaned by mercenary Disgrace of Price.

Cf. Emily Dickinson, *Poems 441, 709 J*[*ohnson*] */ 519, 788 F*[*ranklin*].

Our Taste for the Taboo

Why *had* Orpheus and Lady Lot to turn?
 Due *precisely* to their being warned.

You can count on red balloons to enter thought
At the moment you are cautioned not
 On pain of death (or worse) to entertain
Them. 'Tis the foible of a quirky brain
That from proscriptions we cannot refrain,

 Nor from what's termed *verboten* can abstain.

 Inevitably, then, we shall remain
 At the mercy of Pandora's nasty itch
Which we know better than, but must (God damn it!) scratch.

Away With It

Who call on us to justify *ourselves*?
 Plausibly, justificatory elves,
Whose fay existence may well prove mere hearsay—
Casting self-account in doubt, I daresay.

Purge for Pelf

Neither yard nor the garage we sell,
But what with junk amassed there, might as well.
The warped LPs, half-broken toys, board games,
Old magazines and gilded photo frames,
 Stained ashtrays, training wheels, a goldfish bowl,
 Some matchbox cars, a bucket with a hole,
Are pounced—nay, preyed upon by early birds;
A rite for which I find these silly words
As I perch upon the porch and curse my luck,
And cavil over quarters or a buck.

Incredulously Crass

And now installed for all but one to see,
The funeral parlor's digital marquee.
Date, time, and weather in a bank of lights,
Then (flashing) BUTLER practically indites,
You don't know what you're missing. Garish reminder
Of transience. Try arriving at an unkinder
Display of profit from loss—and if you can,
You better Butler as more tasteless man.

Cropped Out

Hardly high as an elephant's eye—
A muskrat's maybe: green fields of soy.
Though early frost, then sleet, still later, drought
Had cast its maturation into doubt,
The Futures knew this most intrepid bean
(That Illinois, in any case, had seen)
Would thrive during the dog days of August,
And satisfy October hopes of harvest.
 —But staling in silos or under winter stars?
The travesty's not China's; it is ours.

Democratic Doggerel

These be the vilest words Trump's ever heard:
Quid   Pro   Quo;
Latin for lackeys who polish Trump's turd:
Quid   Pro   Quo;
Donald and Rudy and goons from Ukraine
Itching to augment their criminal gain
Wince when we chant this appalling refrain
Redolent of a Republican stain—
Purgative packed with the power to drain
The swamp, and restore calm from chaos again:
Quid   Pro   Quo.

What Moss Can't Cover Up
(*6 August 2019*)

A terrorist, Mideastern and brown-skinned?
I beg to differ, *Prez*, please think again.
Who perpetrate the most heinous crimes,
They hail from the most Caucasian climes.
El Pasoans, Daytonans, rife with sorrow,
Prognosticate the burgs that mourn tomorrow
Those preventable and senseless deaths that come
As surely as the sexton digs their tomb.
(She "died for beauty," he "for truth"—these days
They die from bigots and Republicans' malaise.)

Title; l. 9: Cf. Emily Dickinson, *Poem 1955J[ohnson] / 1998F[ranklin]*.

Climacteric
31 December 2019

Antarctic glaciers melt as this decade ends—
Shall next decade prove too slight to make amends?
Out of sight and mind, the polar thaws
That lend some scientists and cynics pause,
Yet duly conform to disregarded laws
And attest to men's arrogantly fatal flaws,
By deliquescence ominously sign
Our taking for granted Burns' *Auld Lang Syne*.

Not Answering the Bell

Just now I feel the poems knocked out of me.
The Muse my manager's thrown in the towel
Since the cut man, who dresses blows with prosody,
Can't staunch the blood; so in my corner I howl
Like the Great Black Hope who dropped in the fifth round,
Or that Jewish kid with no technique, unsound
At his wit's end, and wheeled off, like Pound
To St. Elizabeth's. Perverse; punch-drunk;
My left and right don't rhyme—poetically, I'm punk.

"the Great Black Hope": Othello; cf. the eponymous tragedy, V.ii.198.

"that Jewish kid…": This reference is merely predicated *from, in no way about* Allan Ginsberg; identification of the caricature *with* him would itself prove quite "unsound," i.e. egregiously unfair to a technically conscientious poet and courageous public figure.

Ezra Pound was, for all intents, incarcerated in St. Elizabeth's Hospital, Washington, D.C., from 1946-58.

Wilmot, of Rochester, Challenged by a Peer

Sir— 'tis mere matter of a flying fuck
I do not deign to give. *Don't* think I care;
My *chef d'oeuvre* intimating, know my pluck
(*Do* read my verse) is founded on despair.
Dare you still throw down your gage to me?
Toss it on my tomb. I died at thirty-three.

"John Wilmot, Earl of Rochester (1648-1681), is one of the few minor poets of the seventeenth century who still seem to have vitality. He was a rake and a foolish young man, who seems to have died of his excesses, but he was also a brilliant stylist who wrote a few memorable poems." –Yvor Winters, *Forms of Discovery* (1967). Rochester's justly lauded ode to nil inscribes his (and our) own fate: "But turn-coat Time assists the foe in vain,...And to thy hungry Womb drives back thy Slaves [all Somethings] again" ("Upon Nothing," VII).

Found on a Flyleaf of *Gulliver's Travels*

Semantically speaking, Houyhnhnms
And Yahoos counterpose as antonyms.
Yet Man and Yahoo prove synonymous;
 Hence, Lemuel come home's a horse's ass—
Where quadrupeds are ridden, whipped, and shot,
Their owners thrive on *saying what is not*,
And Gulliver, aghast, stews in his stable
At the close of Swift's satiric sober fable.

L. 6: In the country of the Houyhnhnms, the very notion of lying defies not only comprehension but definition (cf. Auden, "Words have no word for words that are not true"). Gulliver perforce resorts to circumlocution: to have lied is to have *said the thing which is not*. Cf. *Gulliver's Travels*, IV.iv, v.

Ll. 7-8: Upon his return to England, Gulliver cannot "conceal my antipathy to human kind." Though "I had compelled myself to tolerate the sight of Yahoos,…yet my memory and imaginations were perpetually filled with the virtues and ideas of those exalted Houyhnhmns. And when I began to consider, that by copulating with one of the Yahoo species I had become a parent of more, it struck me with the utmost shame, confusion, and horror.…two young stone-horses, which I keep in a good stable,…understand me tolerably well; I converse with them four hours every day. They are strangers to bridle or saddle; they live in great amity with me, and friendship with each other." Cf. *Gulliver's Travels*, IV.xi; and "A Letter from Capt. Gulliver to His Cousin Sympson": "Have not I the most reason to complain, when I see these very Yahoos carried by Houyhnhnms in a vehicle, as if they were brutes, and those the rational creatures? And indeed to avoid so monstrous and detestable a sight was one principal motive of my retirement hither."

SMALL WONDERS

Equinocturne

Edwin, Letty, Norman, Marcia. Pym's
Autumnal *Quartet*'s poignant magic stems
From tact; from nuanced "fictional harmonics"—
With *Mezzo* often prefixing dynamics,
Staccatos spare and *Tremolos* still more rare.

Sad strains of the quotidian we hear
Confirm subliminal and nascent fears
Of loneliness keynoting later years.
And yet Pym's players counterpoint malaise,
Concluding on a fugue toward further days.

A chamber piece presumes accompaniment:
The score, composed for four, limns her intent.

"*Quartet in Autumn* is a marvel in fictional harmonics." –John Updike.

Upon Looking into Wallace Stevens

The elephant's-ear and grackles skrittered first.
Then Crispin sailed and Canon Aspirin
Took wing on the supremacy of fiction
Wherein fantastic metaphors were nursed.

Even disillusions and the ordinary
Evening instance opportunities for night
Gowns that, although they don't exist, delight
The mind's eye with colors; or a necessary

Angel will unveil the earth anew. He knew
Our rage for order must be satisfied,
Our whims with polysyllables supplied.
And when beyond our view the blackbird flew

To nest in branches on a hither palm,
Imagination thrived, though he'd left the room.

For Edward Lear and Virginia Woolf

'Twas once a kitten queerly plighted troth—
She married, instead of mammocking, a moth.
To stroke rather than strike his fibrous wings
Preoccupied the kitten all that spring.
Her moth in gratitude chirruped a tune
To serenade his feline by the moon
Light bathing both throughout long summer nights:
A most peculiar, most enchanting sight.

Of course, the autumn signified the wane
For one; the other, with instinctive pang,
Desisted from attending to the moth—
Aware, albeit unwittingly, of death.
A tap upon the pane in winter brings
Her intimations of a pair of wings.

"mammocking": Cf. *Coriolanus*, I.iii.65.

Billy Pilgrim's Progress
(In memory of James Ottery)

The Tralfamadorian time warp's all the rage;
Past, present, future failures we assuage.
One does not *climb* the Rockies, just takes in
The range—and mere appraisal means a win.
Beads counted on a string distort the real.
Beads worn in lieu of wrist watches appeal.
Happen upon a moment you deplore?
Dispense with it and take the time next door.
You come out in the end (that's not) a rose
(Though roses have no odor). So it goes.

"All moments, past, present, and future, always have existed, always will exist. The Tralfamadorians can look at all the different moments just the way we look at a stretch of the Rocky Mountains, for instance. They can see how permanent all the moments are, and they can look at any moment that interests them. It is just an illusion we have here on earth that one moment follows another one, like beads on a string, and that once a moment is gone it is gone forever.

"When a Tralfamadorian sees a corpse, all he thinks is that the dead person is in bad condition at that particular moment, but that the same person is just fine in plenty of other moments. Now, when I myself hear that somebody is dead, I simply shrug and say what the Tralfamadorians say about dead people, which is 'So it goes.'"
–from Billy Pilgrim's second letter to the Ilium *News Leader* (in Kurt Vonnegut, *Slaughterhouse Five*).

Ever After, Daddio

West Side Story watched but through the dance
At high school gym (a busy day tomorrow
And it's late) means Jets and Sharks still stand a chance
And Tony and Maria might not sorrow.
Just turn the TV off and go to bed;
No rumble then, *A Place for Them* instead.
And Officer Krupke whistles on his beat
In bliss because no bloodstains mar the street.

On Bernstein, Sondheim, Robbins dim the light,
And bid the gangs and lovers good *Tonight*.

Casa Blancamericana

My father reminisces about a lover
Long departed (silence after speech—not right).
"When Joanne and I recognized that it was over,
We (what the Hell) made love once more despite,
At the convention. And when the early light
Through the window tinctured the queen-size cover,
I said, 'My Dear, we'll always have Detroit.'
And then we went our separate ways in pain—
After sitting side-by-side on the homeward plane.
In the event I encounter my sweetheart's ghost,
To our triste midwestern tryst I'll raise a toast."

L. 2: Cf. Yeats, "After Long Silence."

Musk, Lamp, Memory

"Whoever owned this lamp, he smoked a pipe."—
Or certainly a she it might have been.
Yet recollection prompts imagining
A sage and wizened professorial type
Akin in cast and mien to my old man.

He'd light the lamp to see, and then light up.
The thought he sought was made of sterner stuff
Than first conceived. He drew another puff.
Hence when a shape contrived through intellect took,
Its lineaments were circumscribed by smoke.

Parentheses

He called them *lunulae*, Erasmus did;
Parens, those *little moons* wherein are hid
(Though not so, truly; more so closeted
Without a door, therefore to eyes exposed)
The incidental jewels of our prose.
"Digressions are the life," Sterne's Shandy said.
And those who read Sterne shall, without a doubt,
Attest that Tristram turned all inside out.
Although the Bard surprised the lad and us,
When setting nought therein signed "quietus."
The *lunulae* have suited each extreme—
Or rather, netted both in grammar's stream.

Ll. 6-8: "Digressions, incontestably, are the sun-shine;—they are the life, the soul of reading;—take them out of this book for instance,—you might as well take the book along with them;—one cold eternal winter would reign in every page of it; restore them to the writer;—he steps forth like a bridegroom,—bids All hail; brings in variety, and forbids the appetite to fail." -Laurence Sterne, *The Life and Opinions of Tristram Shandy, Gentlemen* (1759), Vol. I, Ch. xxii.

Ll. 9-10: Cf. Shakespeare's last of the "young man sonnets," number 126.10–14. The "lovely boy"'s fate in effect cashiers Nature's "audit, [which] though delayed answered must be, / And her quietus is to render thee. / ( ) / ( )" Helen Vendler comments that "Inside the parentheses there lies, so to speak, the mute effigy of the rendered youth" (*The Art of Shakespeare's Sonnets* [1997]).

In Praise of Spooner

You've hissed all your mystery lessons, and tasted two
Whole worms. To W.A. we raise a toast:
For who can deny (he's a folly good jello)
That notoriety came at quite a cost.
Yet the local habitation and the name
You endowed justifies allusion to the Bard,
Transposing shame into the key of fame:
 Shakespeare himself wrote, "All that is spoke is marr'd."
And any means of augmenting world laughter
We laud, such as yours—the better, the dafter.

W[illiam] A[rchibald] Spooner (1844-1930), Oxford don, identified with chance solecisms.

L. 5: Cf. *A Midsummer Night's Dream*, V.i.17.

L. 8: Cf. *Othello*, V.ii.357.

Who's Who Was

Will Dawes' and Harry Steinfeldt's absent presence
Via verses where they fail to appear,
Glorify, through Adams' Tinker, Evers, Chance,
And horse heroics of Longfellow's Paul Revere,
Two who, like them, would not stand and wait,
Either at Lexington or at the plate,
But seized the moment; did not hesitate.
For them I cast this couplet of their own
In honor of anonymous renown.

Dawes and Steinfeldt: Tacit actors—patriot and infielder, respectively—who partnered with the men immortalized by Henry Wadsworth Longfellow ("Paul Revere's Ride" [1860]) and Franklin Pierce Adams ("Baseball's Sad Lexicon" [1910]).

The Game's Aglove

It is *Amazing*, and *You Must Believe!*
A recent run sparked seasonal reprieve.
Not since HoJo, Doc, Sid, Kid and Mex
Is enthusiasm justified by Mets
(—Who need rely on Syndegaard and Matz
and Jake deGrom—) who augur that all bets
On last are off. Yet hope renewed, we've learned,
Can but forestall our woe. Forewarned—
Though not forsworn. Destiny or fate for us?
Uncorked champagne or *ignis fatuus*?

L.3: I.e., Howard Johnson, Dwight "Doc" Gooden, Sid Fernandez, Gary Carter, and Keith Hernandez, respectively.

Ll.3-4 unjustly neglect the achievements of the 2000 and 2015 National League champions—who, nevertheless, pale in Gotham lore to the '69 Miracle Mets ("The Amazins"), the '73 comeback crew who rallied round Tug McGraw's mantra ("You Gotta Believe"), and the '86 juggernaut featuring the men mentioned in line 3.

On a Recent Discovery Pertaining to Our Origins
(*for Mark Pence*)

Australopithecus anamensis: Lucy hoist
On prehistoric petard? For who'd dare foist
(Or could, for that matter) a counterfeit skull
As primeval Pia Mater in order to gull
A public just this side of Pleistocene.
Though why would Lucy care to make a scene?
Relieved from the tedium of persiflage
When paleontologists gab about her age.

Reverie, and Homage, at Thirty Thousand Feet

When the plane penetrates above opacous clouds
 Our flight converts to Arctic Circle voyage.
White at the wings' (now port and starboard's) edge
 Intimates ice that our frigid vessel ploughs
On its trek to a reputedly unchartered pole—
 For time as well as space suffers a whole
Fanciful recasting; and albeit absurd,
 My mind's eye enlists with Rear Admiral Byrd.
I pray, too, that my real journey's end
 Concludes as his, once we commence our descent.
Whether in fact first reaching South *and* North,
 Byrd always returning safe conferred more worth.

Ironically in the context of this tribute, Richard E. Byrd actually directed his arctic expeditions from the air. That he flew over the North Pole is disputed.

Taingeil Dhut, **P.M.D.**

Interluding for *The Yellow Cake Revue*,
The Stromness chords sound strummed; for Davies knew
An elegy opposing mining metal,
To touch the heart, took tapping on the pedal.
He penned his piece to lend the Orkneys aid
As caveat: a farewell serenade.

Peter Maxwell Davies composed *The Yellow Cake Revue* suite (1980) in protest against proposed uranium quarrying near Stromness, a town on the largest of the Orkney Islands. (The Scots Secretary of State denied the petition to mine.) "Farewell to Stromness," the lovely third piece in the suite, written for unaccompanied piano, has been aptly transcribed for guitar.

Translation
(for Cameron and Kara McElwrath)

Turning toward her, turning back on Young,
Whose voice betrays his emptiness of mouth.
What can a tow-haired toked Canadian
Conceive of charms that typify my South?

It's true, we've erred in loving evil men,
And lied about "necessity" perhaps.
Yet conscience cannot haunt about back then;
Next time we'll place our faith in better chaps.

Strong shoals and swampers serenade our woes
With blues and ballads that convey so much,
Alleviating Mason-Dixon lows.
Moonshine for poultice lends a local touch.

Ain't no place like Sweet Alabaman Home:
Wisteria and red clay beneath blue dome.

Cf. Lynyrd Skynyrd, "Sweet Home Alabama."

First Little Piggy

Champagne, and chicken thighs (a pack of them);
Some parsley, sage—no rosemary this time;
A yellow rose with elongated stem,
And avocados to complete the rhyme.
Meow Mix for the puss, some tins of fish
To supplement her dry food in the dish—
A combination cats devoutly wish.
Those croutons in the cabinet are stale.
Some bean dip also while you're in that aisle,
And hearts of palm. Let's pass, though, on the kale,
Which in our fridge would merely rot to waste:
I shall not purchase what I cannot taste.
Enough. It's true what Williams told Mike Wallace,
That even in Hyvee the Muse might call us.

Cf. the dialogue in William Carlos Williams, *Paterson IV* (223): "Q. Now, that sounds just like a fashionable grocery list! A. Yes. Anything is good material for poetry. Anything. I've said it time and time again."
L. 7: Cf. *Hamlet*, III.i.62.

Two Faults

The art of parking's blasted hard to master—
Though (*pace* Bishop), never in my keep,
The loss of it proves but a moot disaster.
Still, parallels and curbs disturb my sleep.
The auto gods, moreover, have devised,
Should I stop on a hill, my steep demise:
For never can I fix the parking brake
Sufficiently for frictive force to take.
Hence, woe to those below in Mazda's wake.
(My wife thinks even driving's my mistake.)

Cf. Elizabeth Bishop, "One Art." IN NO WAY is my poem intended as pastiche or parody of Bishop's poignant masterpiece.

The Geese at UIS
(who congregate in Parking Lot E)

The University geese flock not to class,
Yet strut peripatetic just the same.
Though if the truth be told—well then, alas,
These fowls resemble us in more than name.
For when they honk, or haggle over food,
Their feathers, index finger-like, protrude
In accusation or defense, or both;
As when faculty members long in tooth
(Or not so old, still dallying with youth,
Albeit tenured) justify a rant or tiff,
Because their colleague-rivals pecked and sniffed.
(No doubt, they're not "The Wild Swans at Coole"—
The gaggle, though, of egos at our school,
Elicit likenings with which to fool.)

Small Wonder

It's true, some people *do* look like their dogs.
The college co-ed years don't yet betray,
In the quad at noon, airing her Irish Setter,
Resembles her in spirit more than letter—
Their pride and youth and sheen embrace the day.
But my neighbor in diurnal dialogues
With his Jack Russell ("Phoebe." *Bark*.
"Yes, Phoebe." *Bark*.)—their eyes and jutting jaws,
Their miens indubitably bear a stark
Similitude that gives me puzzled pause.
(And summons, silent as bemused, applause.)

Tuesday (not the Third Day)

Torpid anticipation blent with dread:
The recyclist's wheels summon me from bed.
Now empty crates conveyed to the front porch
Await a week's replenishment of plastic,
Tin cans, wine bottles, newspapers, and such
Related transient dregs. Somewhat fantastic
On reflection, all the detritus we toss.
Though Shakespeare notes we increase store with loss.
Some things somehow return. What's in the bin
Might (as I hope to) tomorrow rise again.

L. 8: Cf. *Sonnet 64*.8.

What Beats All

Today the wind chimes tolled to mind John Murry,
 Percussionist in Hampshire High School's band,
Who beat his down beat up in harried hurry
 As though to close the gap 'twixt self and stand;
Or (for John seemed a gentlemanly bloke)
 Deferred his triangle or cow bell stroke
Until his mates had finished their own measure
(Again, in friendship, not desire for leisure).
'Tis forty years before if 'tis a day,
And retrospect obliges me to say
That, given Murry's choice of instrument,
Of all who marched, or mangled some event,
John never, while flat brass, sharp woodwinds crooned,
Could be arraigned for playing out of tune.

What Goes Round

The urban cyclists astonish me.
The graceful, death-defying intricacy
With which they weave through traffic at top speed,
Evading potholes that they hardly heed;
Unhelmeted, as though defying fear
(A choice that seems absurdly cavalier),

Amazes less with their unnerved exploits
Than by reminding *me* once thus adroit,
So many years ago as wheels have spokes.
Hence, which prognosticates that by the looks
Of things, since memory attests I live,
These daredevils are likely to survive.

Motions Recollected in Tranquility

I wandered lonely 'long Melinda Lane
As solitary as a single cloud
In blue sky absent any threat of rain;
Then all at once I heard a whizzing loud
Of bicyclists in squadron-like formation
(Occasion for this stroller's consternation).

Continuous as those dancing daffodils
Immortalized in quaint Wordsworthian measure—
I'd lie to say their wheels lent keen pleasure;
Though can concede this reminiscence fills
An idle April evening's solitude,
And stocks with thought a prior vacant mood.

Title: Cf. Wordsworth, "Preface" to *Lyrical Ballads* (1802): "Poetry is the spontaneous overflow of powerful feelings: it takes its origin from emotion recollected in tranquility." The paradox of this dictum always strikes me.

L. 8 *et seriatim*: Cf. Wordsworth, "I wandered Lonely as a Cloud."

Ll. 10–12: Cf. in addition to Wordsworth's closing stanza, Eliot, "La Figlia que Piange": "Sometimes these cogitations still amaze The troubled midnight and the noon's repose."

Done (Donne): Gone

Last night my old Rolex ran out of time:
Perhaps not precisely at seven past the hour
If entropy already drained some power
Through the years of *ticking ticking ticking*—to limn
"The measure of motion" (Donne); a task sublime
If in the grandest scheme of things construed.
Though perched upon my wrist a chore subdued
To the petty pacing of one man's routine:
An owner who, like Time, outlasted it,
Yet someday shall himself no longer watch,
Nor from Time's whirligigs attempt to snatch
As his revenge on It a fetch of wit—
Since like my watch I share a dire fate
Of one day needing no excuse for running late.

L. 5: Cf. *Devotions Upon Emergent Occasions*, XIV. Donne "consider[ed] time to be *but* the measure of motion" (italics mine); yet I have always marveled at this function of the dimension; and the Dean acknowledges that "this imaginary half-nothing time be of the essence of our happiness."

L. 8: Cf. *Macbeth*, V.v.23.

Ll. 11-2: Cf. *Twelfth Night*, V.i.399.

Near Sugarloaf

At dawn the paths by old New England farms
Confer on me perambulating peace—
As though, put out to pasture, false alarms
Or real harms, chew cud and kneel and cease
Perturbing. "There and then or here and now,"
The meadows ask, "why milk a colic cow?"

Strange Meeting

I met another trooper by the highway,
Among the ones who toiled for all the states.
We chatted by the stop light where he waits.
"Thank you," he said, but that I ought to say,
And so I did. "You know," he might have said,
"In Vietnam when I was pumped with lead,
They pinned another heart upon my chest
And sent me home—'Well done, son'—*home* to rest.
And here I stand, with honors all discharged.
Impoverished, tricked, sick, hungry, and at large."
That monologue's imagined melodrama;
Unconscionably real, his homeless trauma.
He only answered me, "I'd serve again."
And then the light that let us meet turned green.

Cf. Wilfred Owen, "Strange Meeting."

Semper Fraternitas

Brick and ivy's tacit brotherhood
Is writ in green upon apartment walls.
Timeless, ubiquitously understood
From Wrigley Field to hallowed Harvard halls.
When at world's end the final trumpets blow,
And the aftermath takes *almost* all in tow,
There can't *but*, by some thirteenth hour order,
Remain a sprig wrapped round two bricks and mortar.

ABOUT THE POET

ETHAN LEWIS, Professor Emeritus of English at the University of Illinois-Springfield, has authored seven previous books: with Robert Kuhn McGregor, an Edgar Allan Poe Award-winning monograph on Dorothy L. Sayers, *Conundrums for the Long Weekend* (Kent State UP 2000); and, published by Cambridge Scholars Press, *Modernist Image* (2010), *Reflexive Poetics* (2012), *The Shakespeare Project and Ensuing Essays* (2015), *Literary Nuances: Millions of Strange Shadows* (2018), *Literary Essays: On Explicable Splendours* (2020), and *Modern Sonneteers, Hilary Mantel, and Critical Letters: A Triptych* (2021. The last three books, like this one, were typeset by Mark Pence.). His work has appeared in several venues—including, on multiple occasions, *Paideuma*, *Spring* (journals of the Ezra Pound and E.E. Cummings Societies, respectively), *South Dakota Review*, *University of Mississippi Studies in English*, and *Papers of the International Symbolist Conference*. His chapter on "Imagism" is compassed in *The Cambridge Companion to Ezra Pound*. *Take Fives* constitutes the yield of a pleasing poetic renascence after a nearly two decades' lull since last he cast a line in love or anger, or even equanimity.

AN APOLOGIA BY WAY OF AFTERWORD,
for have the poems not stood on their own merits, this Defense ought be dismissed.

Though an English professor for close on thirty years now, I'm not "an academic poet," hence will never alienate an audience with abstrusities and hyper-theoretical preoccupations. I note thus with all due respect to the fine cadre of Academic Poets. I'm just not one of their ilk, and so not subject to their pitfalls. As a peculiarly paradoxical attestation to my non-Academism: I can rarely write a lick of free verse.

  Which segues to lobbying more positively. Most readers, I've found, hunger for "the emotion embracing efficacy of rhyme and meter,"* particularly when these devices envelop wit*ful* (vis-à-vis merely witty) *clearly expressed* sophistication—that combination of form and content engages and entertains; and that's my métier. Not academic, I am, though, literary—and authors in various genres at times figure as allusory matrices or even personages in my poems. (Their presence accounted for in innocuously informative notes—i.e., no daunting *Waste Land*-esque scholia.) The appearance of these artists is explained by the spectrum of my experience: what Borges stated about many of the most vivid moments in his life coming through encounters with art applies to me also—and, I'd venture, to a sizeable readership.

  Given *that* predilection, my audience would plausibly likewise approve, and *co-respond with*, my *use of poetry as*

---

*David Lehman, lauding Philip Larkin.

a means of thinking—as *understanding through literally coming to terms*—or at the very least, by that process comprehending sympathetically the incapacity to understand. Wittgenstein writes: "If you look at something in the correct way, then you will comprehend it." Poetic form functions for me as corrective vision—not only in writing, but, more, in reading poetry; which augurs how I hope (as so many poets have for me), via verses, "to help people live their lives." Quoting Wallace Stevens:

> What is [the poet's] function? Certainly it is not to lead people out of the confusion in which they find themselves. Nor is it…to comfort them while they follow their leaders to and fro. [Certainly not! Never *not* more so than now.] [H]is function is to make his imagination theirs, and…he fulfills himself only as he sees his imagination become the light in the minds of others. His role, in short, is to help people live their lives…because the poet has quickened [the audience], has educed from it that for which it was searching in itself and in the life around it, and which it had not yet quite found.
> ("The Noble Rider and the Sound of Words")

CODA:
Mid-Length Playfully Personal Study in Pentameter

Late December 2021

Today, the first of my retirement,
Passed the placard, *Welcome to U.I.S.*,
And wondered what that sign to me now meant.
I did not leave *for cause*, nor from duress.
It's not that I'm no longer *Welcome* there.
Yet even so, as though I've disappeared.

I tell myself, *Relax, old boy, do chill.*
No reason, nay no right, to stew or fret.
The mirror testifies you're visible,
A mist upon the glass, you're not dead yet.
But that nursery rhyme keeps mumming in my ear
About encountering the man who wasn't there.

A call from Corrine Frisch (beloved), my ex-.
"How are you?" "I'm okay. And you [*Brute*]?"
The fault (*JC* again) is mine: no sex.
It's not in stars to legislate one's duty.[1]
At issue, honestly, no "obligation";
Although *amour* remains, absence of passion.

---

1. The fault, dear Brutus, is not in the stars,
   But in ourselves, that we are underlings. –*Julius Caesar*, I.ii.140.

Go figure. Then again, don't even try.
Absurdity's the rule, writes sage Camus.
But that dictates our futile fathoming why,
Hence, speculation on this matter's due
To confirm the other facet of absurd:
The *world's* irrationality, in a word.[2]

Where went the magic? Or was it ever there?
I've never been *l'homme moyen sensuale*.
Physicality for me prompts fear;
Mere prospect of a touch can make me ill.
Yet oft enough, the female flesh allured:
A paradox partaking of absurd.

Loss plausibly stemming from compromised health.
Endocarditas: a bleak metaphor.
I pump artificially—sort of by stealth.
Lacking in Yeatsean *deep heart's core*?[3]
Okay then! With *reasons for* I've had enough.
Subsequent stanzas address other stuff.

---

2. "I said that the world is absurd, but I was too hasty. This world in itself is not reasonable, that is all that can be said. But what is absurd is the confrontation of this irrational and the wild longing for clarity whose call echoes in the human heart. The absurd depends as much on man as on the world. For the moment it is all that links them together. It binds them one to the other as only hatred can weld two creatures together." –Albert Camus, *The Myth of Sisyphus* [1955], trans, Justin O'Brien (New York: Vintage International, 2018), 21.

3. Cf. W.B. Yeats, "The Lake Isle of Innisfree."

Better tread the course of pavements grey.[4]
Safer, and consistent with my mood.
To inevitable reasoning I've paid
My dues, now on irrationals can duly brood.
Or rather, muse upon what I've discovered;
Solitary, somewhat free, de-lovered.

Now what I shall disclose requires disclaimer
Lest I be thought inane, insane, quite daft.
Lest my fair lady reader scoff—who'd blame her?
Lest my incredulous gentleman reader laugh.
Good ladies and gentlemen, *pace* your lest;
My *Eureka*'s limit is manifest.

Subjective reconcilement of time and space,
Though it confirm, in spirit, relativity,
In laudatory annals owns no place,
Proves but a boon to private sensitivity.
One wants to share; yet a boast would be absurd.
So knowing that I know that, rest assured.

According to the good Dean Doctor Donne,
Whose poetry *and* prose I so esteem,
Time is merely the measure of motion[5]:
A neat conceit for mantra or for meme—
Which since some forty-odd years past I read,
Sounds intermittently within my head.

---

4. Ibid.
5. John Donne, *Devotions Upon Emergent Occasions*, "Meditation XIV."

Only with this Autumn Term near end
(Hence what that consequence for me entailed)
Could I Donne's haunting resonance apprehend
Where heretofore just why it stuck I failed
To discern. Yet when time's viewed as but a means,
One may not garner how that view demeans

The element, which more than *merely* measures,
But itself is reckoned for its length, and weighed.
Ignore time numbering 'mongst time's chiefest treasures,
Its *embodiment*, our time, is then betrayed.
I would permanently frame the claim in rhyme:
To have discovered sacred space—the place—of time!

Before, I'd drive to school. *I've class at six.*
Time measures motion *toward*, then *of*, that aim.
Yet severance of instrument from object was fixed;
Obtuseness to potential one-and-same.
Back then, at school, with spouse, I'd *be* somewhere.
And now, my *forward then*'s my only *there*.

Then is there. I lay me down to sleep
And fancy have embarked upon a quest.
My bed's a plane, dirigible, or ship,
Or (under covers) submarine: last best.
I soar time's skies, or scour temporal seas;
Lay anchor on the moments *where* I please.

When is where. A horologue's a map.
One arrives at eight-fifteen *on* eight-fifteen,
As well as whenwhere circumstances hap
On any chrono-locale in between.
And at each port of call 'twixt sleep and wake,
Mind's eye observes, deduces, even makes.

Moreover, future's undiscovered country—
A better bourn than Hamlet theorized.[6]
And always beckoning, since every sundry
Once-then-now clears path for new surmise.
Thus with such musings I enliven nights,
Enthralled by Kairos geographic heights.

So fine. Though on the pavement grey of day
And the quotidian, I must confess
Convention dictates *be somewhere*. Anyway,
By day, at wit's end, I'm a silly mess.
In fact, it feels as if *I've disappeared*—
Absently manifesting *man not there*.

I've work, of course—retired in part to write
On passions that demanded their just due;
Devoting my interpretative might
To lettered heroes: Milton and Camus.
Toward limning nuances in English epic,
And implications of absurdist ethic.

---

6. I.e., death, or plausibly "something after death, Th' undiscovered country from whose bourn No traveler returns" (*Hamlet*, III.i.78).

Still, late December winds whisper *alone*,
And solitary study takes its toll
Though it rewards—three months since you have gone,
Covid of course confines, and I've left school.
Absurd? Hardly—"see whole" the situation;
Confront it "steadily"—"life"'s isolation.

Matthew Arnold "To a Friend"[7]: *steadily and whole*;
Though things seen depend as much on the perceiver,[8]
On not one's eyes in this case, but the soul,
Whose tangent thoughts too typically deceive her.
Of what I feel I could take possession
Better were it not for damned obsession

About that or this, the "one thing or another,"
The ruminative flavor of the day.
Although I might prefer the fretful bother
Over emptiness that fretting keeps at bay.
I stare abstracted at the PC screen,
Mumbling mindlessly these lines again.

Must needs recall how fortunate I am.
Two thousand miles east an older man
With whom I share a history and surname,
Wrestles with most all but cannot stand.
And hours from that *agon*, his one-time wife,
Bereft of memory, lives loss of life.

---

7. Specifically, to Sophocles, "The mellow glory of the Attic stage," "Who saw life steadily and saw it whole."
8. Cf. Wallace Stevens, *Adagia*: "Things seen are things as seen. Absolute real."

Come February, I shall see them both
And Dad's caretaker, friend, ex-lover, Jane,[9]
To whom I'm so indebted, yet am loathe,
From guilt and shame, to thank *too* much. Fain
Would I return to Boston—but alas,
I lack the courage (not to mention, cash).

But when (next year?) we do sell this *abode*—
Fancifully past tense of *we abide*,
Having dispensed with matrimonial mode,
You downtown with him, while here I hide
In back-room, bedroom-study, library,
A nook for writing and for reverie—

What then?...

What *then*? Of *now*, at least, I've little doubt
That now will pass as now's to come will pass.
"By indirections find directions out"[10]
I shall—and a proposit, a la *Lycidas*,
On eve of soon now 2022:
"Tomorrow to fresh woods and pastures new."

---

9. Not her actual name. But the exigencies of semantics and rhyme coalesce (even regardless of scruples ensuing from confidentiality). What I meant to state and sound could not accord with "Martha"—though not for lack of trying. *Videlicit* this rejected draft:

    Come February, I shall see them both
    And Dad's caretaker, friend, ex-lover Martha,
    To whom I'm so indebted, yet am loathe,
    From shame, to thank too much. Were I Siddhartha,
    I could recompense. By calm, through "Om,"
    That sacred word, move home: aid Dad *and* Mom.

Yet let the last words be Albert Camus'
(Assist from Dante): "creativity"
When mid "dark wood," to one's soul self
Is due, as "evidence of man's sole dignity."
Emotions versed herein, resisting thesis,
Lent feeling form: summed poetry's "*ascesis*."[11]

---

10. Cf. *Hamlet*, II.i.63. Polonius' prescription can apply to better ends than his own—to Milton's meanderings in "Lycidas," for example.
11. Cf. *The Myth of Sisyphus*, 115; *Inferno*, Canto I.1: "*Nel mezzo del cammin di nostra vita / mi ritrovai per una selva oscura, / che la dir-itta via era smarrita.*"